The Part-Time Teacher

Judy Wells

Rainy Day Women Press
P.O. Box 1085
Willits, CA 95490

Printed in the United States of America

Dedication:

This book is dedicated to my colleagues, that great horde of part-time teachers, those who quit and those who carried on, and all the students we ever taught.

With loving thanks to my family—
Irene, Melinda, Nancy, Mel—and
particularly to my dear friend Bridget Connelly.

CONTENTS

I.

ADMINISTRATION

2 The part-time teacher is jealous of other starting part-time teachers

3 The part-time teacher wonders whether she will have a job each semester

4 The part-time teacher does not like her contract

5 The part-time teacher wants to start a union

6 The part-time teacher calls in sick

7 The part-time teacher meets her cousins in the mailroom

8 The part-time teacher sneaks xerox copies

9 The part-time teacher is fired from her night job

II.

STUDENTS (VOLUNTARY):

CREATIVE WRITING

11 The part-time teacher's students explain their muses

12 The part-time teacher has a pet

13 The part-time teacher wonders whether she should take cpr

14 The part-time teacher has a self-effacing genius in her class

15 The part-time teacher is at her wit's end

16 The part-time teacher talks with her night students about publishing

17 The part-time teacher organizes a field trip

18   The part-time teacher's 85 year old student gets rebellious at times

19   The part-time teacher teaches a women's course in the 80s

21   The part-time teacher learns her students want to heal themselves

22   The part-time teacher discusses her students while her mate sleeps

III.

STUDENTS (INVOLUNTARY):

ENGLISH IA

24   The part-time teacher uses the passive voice

25   The part-time teacher sometimes fears for her students' lives

27   The part-time teacher teaches a unit from the *Borzoi College Reader* called "Cultures In Tension"

29   The part-time teacher is a white woman

31   The part-time teacher gets in hot water teaching Alice Walker

34   The part-time teacher decides to stand up for herself

35   The part-time teacher presents her final argument for *The Color Purple* and the strong black woman responds

36   The white part-time teacher and the strong black woman have an eye to eye confrontation

38   The part-time teacher deals with mutiny

39   The part-time teacher has a scam run on her

40   The part-time teacher accuses a jock of plagiarizing

41   The part-time teacher's English IA students discuss homosexuality

43   The part-time teacher observes a black male and white male testing their machismo on each other

45   The part-time teacher is hungry
46   The part-time teacher has advanced degrees and no IRA
47   The part-time teacher reads Melville

IV.

PERSONAL

49   The part-time teacher does not keep horses
50   The part-time teacher needs a benefactor
51   The part-time teacher meets a woman in the woods who tells her a story
52   The part-time teacher is examined with a fine tooth comb
53   The part-time teacher believes there is a conspiracy against women's poetry classes
55   The part-time teacher's boyfriend tells her she should get out of the systemand run her own business
57   The part-time teacher meets a fellow traveler
59   The part-time teacher asks herself why she teaches part-time
60   The part-time teacher re-examines her answers why she teaches part-time

The
Part-
Time
Teacher

I.

ADMINISTRATION

THE PART-TIME TEACHER IS JEALOUS OF OTHER STARTING PART-TIME TEACHERS

The part-time teacher is jealous of other starting part-time teachers who appear so perky and happy and satisfied. They teach ESL and business math. They have many students. They do not teach poetry.

The part-time teacher remembers being thrilled to get hired 3 years before. She had not taught in 10 years. She was glad she found a school which did not ask many questions, accepted her degrees, and did not sniff at her Ph.D. She remembered asking the Chair at another community college for a job in the English Department. The Chair found her resume in a file. She held it up by one corner and said, "I don't know why I still have this. This is the kind of resume I usually toss into the wastebasket." The part-time teacher was sick of being so overqualified that she was tossed into the wastebasket and had to get a job as a clerk.

Now the part-time teacher feels she is underqualified for her job. She feels she ought to be a trained psychiatrist, social worker, and linguist. She feels she ought to be a skilled publicist, a racial arbiter, and a sex therapist. She feels she ought to be a battered wives counselor, a union organizer, and a professional Mommy and Daddy. She feels as if her ego is understaffed.

THE PART-TIME TEACHER WONDERS WHETHER SHE WILL HAVE A JOB EACH SEMESTER

The part-time teacher breaks out in hives 2 days before school starts. Last year it was diarrhea. The full-time teachers wonder how she stays so thin. She wonders whether 20 students have signed up for her creative writing course.

Sometimes the full-time teachers send strange, new, and interesting students into her course to help her enrollment. They usually look terrified and bewildered when she begins to talk about Theodore Roethke or Diane Wakoski or Tolstoy. They thought they were going to a basic grammar course. They disappear after the first class, sweating profusely and promising to return.

THE PART-TIME TEACHER DOES NOT LIKE HER CONTRACT

The part-time teacher is asked to sign a contract which says she will give up her course to a full-time faculty member if he or she needs it. Every time she reaches that section, she balks. No, I will not give up my course to a full-time faculty member, she says. Absolutely not. I won't. This has never happened. Still, the part-time teacher does not want to sign her contract. "Thanks for your cooperation," says the contract.

The part-time teacher wonders whether electricians or grape pickers would sign a contract signing away their jobs. She wonders why hundreds of part-time teachers sitting at home at their desks, pens poised above their contracts, do not refuse to sign on the dotted line. She wonders whether she ought to call in the California Self-Esteem Task Force and ask them what is wrong.

THE PART-TIME TEACHER WANTS TO START A UNION

The part-time teacher goes to a meeting whose subject is IMPROVING SUPPORT FOR PART-TIME TEACHERS. The administrator spends the first 15 minutes telling the part-time teachers about the chain of command at the college. He says the President is God. "Goddess," corrects the speech teacher. The President is a woman.

Next, part-time teachers complain about not being able to xerox 30 copies of handouts for their students. They are only allowed 20 copies for 30 students. The administrator adjusts his rimless glasses, looks handsome and suave, and grants them 10 more copies.

The part-time teacher meditates on the memo she has already sent the administrator. "Ten extra copies are nice, but need I remind you that it would be very supportive of you to offer us health insurance and eligibility for unemployment, extra pay for office hours, a real contract, and a guaranteed key to the ladies' room?"

He promises parking permits and posters, bandaids for cancer.

THE PART-TIME TEACHER CALLS IN SICK

The part-time teacher jumps into her car one rainy morning.

It refuses to turn over. She calls the secretary and reports: "Unless something drastic happens in the next ten minutes, I won't be there this morning." She returns to her car. No dice. She calls the secretary again and reports: "I won't be in." "And what shall I say is the reason?" asks the secretary tactfully. The part-time teacher must lie. There is no death in the family. She needs that $30. She has rehearsed her lie. "Just say illness." "All right," says the secretary.

The part-time teacher feels slightly guilty even though she has not been absent for 212 years. She remembers one of her poetry students who reported having a breakdown when she was 30. Her psychiatrist said to her: "Miss Eliot, why do you always tell the truth? You must learn to tell white lies like everyone else." The part-time teacher still feels guilty. She coughs.

THE PART-TIME TEACHER MEETS HER COUSINS IN THE MAILROOM

The part-time teacher discovers she has two very distant cousins at her college. They are all part-time teachers. They are all descendants of the Dickinson line which also spawned Emily. Two are writers; one wants to be. They all teach English.

The part-time teacher calls one of the women "Cousin" who reminds her of a family member because she's angry all the time about just who screwed her over today in the writing center.

Her "Cousin" brings her a biography of Emily Dickinson, and they wonder whether the poet had agoraphobia. The part-time teacher thinks a streak of it runs in her family. Her father lived one block from his mother's home in the same small town where he was born. The part-time teacher herself hates to move. She is often forced to, but she clings to her room and her curtains as she goes. She clings to her job, though she knows it's a losing proposition and has been since Prop. 13.

Should she stay in the college market and get phobic? Or should she stay in her room like Emily and write poems.

THE PART-TIME TEACHER SNEAKS
XEROX COPIES

The part-time teacher uses the xerox machine in the faculty room. She turns it on and presto she makes copies of her syllabus. Unfortunately, the secretary appears out of nowhere even though it is night. "I won't tell your secret," she says, eyeing the machine, but the next week when the part-time teacher turns on the machine, nothing happens. The paper trays have disappeared from the machine. The cabinets are locked.

The secretary is taking a real estate course. The part-time teacher wonders whether she should cancel her class and go into real estate herself. She wonders whether she should apply for the secretary's job. The part-time teacher peeks into the real estate course as she goes to her poetry class. It is packed with attentive men and women with eager notebooks. She glances at the scrawny string of 8 potential creative writers on her roster. She wonders where she went wrong.

THE PART-TIME TEACHER IS FIRED
FROM HER NIGHT JOB

The part-time teacher has thirteen students in her creative writing course. She needs seven more people. The students discuss getting bogus bodies into the course. One high schooler wants to sign up four of her friends. High school students only have to pay $1.00. We will pretend they are in the course. Everyone thinks this is a good idea. Unfortunately, the administrator arrives during the discussion of bogus bodies. He is a nice man. The part-time teacher once dreamed she was dating him. He axes her course. He is not a nice man.

The students gather round her after class for support. They would like to fight. Their new goal in life is to take a cancelled course. The part-time teacher is pooped. She would just like to go home.

Instead, she goes to Carrow's with three students to talk about poetry. She decides to order apple pie with vanilla ice cream. The waiter comes and says there is no vanilla ice cream. Sorry. The part-time teacher would like to wring his neck.

She goes home. Pounds her pillow, pummels her boyfriend to sleep with words he does not remember the next day. She pees all night. At dawn, the part-time teacher pounds *The Part-Time Teacher* poems into her typewriter.

II.

STUDENTS (VOLUNTARY):

CREATIVE WRITING

THE PART-TIME TEACHER'S STUDENTS
EXPLAIN THEIR MUSES

The part-time teacher has a re-entry woman in her
creative writing class who says she listens to music
under her pillow at night. It gives her strange and
wondrous dreams which enhance her creativity. She
is excited and bobs her head like a sleepless bird.

In the second class, the re-entry woman tells the part-
time teacher that she has a machine she puts under
her pillow which can record her thoughts.
"WOOOOOOOOO," say the other class members.
"It's true," says the re-entry woman.

Another woman says, "I get my plays from my
dreams. Last night two lines came to me in my sleep.
I said to myself, I don't want to roll over and wake
my husband just for two lines. But then a woman ap-
peared and said, 'If you don't write them down,
you'll never get them back.' So I got up and put them
down. I don't have no machines."

The part-time teacher wishes she had a woman dicta-
tor in her dreams.

THE PART-TIME TEACHER HAS A PET

The part-time teacher's favorite student is a re-entry woman with coal black hair. She wears a different colored outfit to every class: yellow sweatshirt, yellow pants, and yellow tennies; red sweatshirt, red pants, and red tennies. She sends the part-time teacher notes in orange envelopes on turquoise, red, and purple squares of paper. Once, for a party, she boiled eggs and colored them red, blue, and purple, and set them in matching nests of pink.

She writes perfect sonnets on her wordprocessor and ballads. She never speaks except to read her poems, but her eyes say more than all the mouths in the class. She likes Anne Sexton, has survived several husbands, numerous religions and sons, cancer, and a secretarial stint. Her new man, 14 years younger than she, lets her stay home and write.

THE PART-TIME TEACHER WONDERS WHETHER SHE SHOULD TAKE CPR

The part-time teacher has an 85 year old student. He has been taking classes for 20 years. The younger students wonder whether he will die in the course. His two favorite critical statements are: "Your poem doesn't have a title." and "That's not poetry." He is usually right.

THE PART-TIME TEACHER HAS A SELF-EFFACING GENIUS IN HER CLASS

She is a woman. She is overweight and crippled and she creeps to class on canes, but her mind soars over the universe for subjects. She's been Jack London and Beethoven and the smallest atom in the atmosphere. She's been a prehistoric turtle and she's made love to the stars.

She's too good for the *New Yorker* and the *Atlantic Monthly*; perhaps that's the reason she will not publish. The part-time teacher sees her as the Emily Dickinson of Richmond, the belle of San Pablo, while her other students scratch their heads.

THE PART-TIME TEACHER IS AT HER WIT'S END

The part-time teacher has a cheerful madman in her class. She finally discerns he is a playwright. She thinks he creates great dialogue from his voices, but he goes on too long. She sees a packet of 10 single-spaced pages. He is only on page 2. On party days, he brings popcorn, which he pops in class, and passes out in individual brown paper bags. The part-time teacher does not get any. On the subject of mothers, he says: "When I take one tranquilizer, she tells me to take 2. When I take two tranquilizers, she tells me to take 3. When I take three tranquilizers, she tells me to take 4." He lives at home. He talks all the time. The part-time teacher wants him to take 5.

THE PART-TIME TEACHER TALKS WITH HER NIGHT STUDENTS ABOUT PUBLISHING

Most of the part-time teacher's night students are not interested in publishing. They are in her class for other reasons. Their husbands have committed suicide. They need 3 more units of credit to get into CAL. They have always had an urge to write. They want to meet a woman. They may try to publish later. They may never try to publish.

Only the 85 year old student says: "Absolutely I want to publish. I'm too old to wait until I'm older!"

The part-time teacher laughs. She likes the crotchety old man because he is the only poet she knows who has called Death a punched out BART ticket.

THE PART-TIME TEACHER ORGANIZES
A FIELD TRIP

The part-time teacher invites her students to see a
play on Jack Kerouac in Oakland in which she will
read her own poetry. One student shows up. He is
hovering around the refreshment table before the
play begins. The part-time teacher's boyfriend thinks
the student is the actor playing Jack Kerouac.

The part-time teacher, her boyfriend, and the student
sit on folding chairs in a line as the play begins. The
actor playing Jack Kerouac lifts up a bottle of booze at
the end of Scene i. The student disappears from the
room. He returns with three paper cups of wine and
lines them up under his chair. In the intermission, he
begins an animated discussion with the part-time
teacher's boyfriend and falls off his chair. The part-
time teacher is embarrassed.

In Act II, the student begins to talk loudly, "When are
you going to read your poems?" The part-time
teacher scrunches down in her folding chair. The stu-
dent lurches off and does not return. She reads her po-
ems without him.

He does not come to the next class, but returns to the
one after that. He walks down the hall with her after
class and promises: "I'm really sorry. It won't happen
again." She wonders just how many others he has
said this to.

THE PART-TIME TEACHER'S 85 YEAR OLD STUDENT GETS REBELLIOUS AT TIMES

The part-time teacher forgets one Tuesday that her 85 year old student signed up to read a story in her creative writing class. She apologizes and promises to let him read his story on Thursday.

On Thursday there is a woman ahead of him who is going to present a play. The 85 year old man looks at her manuscript darkly and says, "This'll take a half an hour."

"No, it won't," says the playwright. "It goes really fast once you start reading it." The 85 year old man is silent.

A half hour later, the old man starts reading his story. It is an imitation Hemingway, with two men who talk about booze, guns, lack of women, and an old father who is outside in the woods somewhere with a gun. A shotgun blast goes off at the end of the story.

"DOES THE STORY HAVE A SINGLE EFFECT?" demands the old man. "DOES THE WEATHER HAVE AN EFFECT ON THE STORY?" He blasts one question after another, his eyes on fire. There is no space for an answer.

THE PART-TIME TEACHER TEACHES A WOMEN'S COURSE IN THE 80s

The part-time teacher teaches a women's poetry course on the side in a university. Three men show up and are the most active students in the course. The part-time teacher wonders why, but remembers this is Berkeley where men show up for a woman's course. The woman who was the most eager to take the course drops it.

One man is always the first student when the part-time teacher arrives. "Am I welcome here?" he asks the first day. "I don't know," she laughs. He is a psychologist; she wonders why he is taking the course. Does he want to peg women? Does he want to date someone in the course? He always looks embarrassed.

The part-time teacher gives the students handouts of Susan Griffin's poems. The female students do not like her poems and do not like her anger. One gentle man identifies. The part-time teacher reads an angry Griffin poem aloud:

> AN ANSWER TO A MAN'S QUESTION
> "WHAT CAN I DO ABOUT WOMEN'S
> LIBERATION?"

> Wear a dress.

Smiles begin to crack around the room.

> Find a job.

Iron your dress.

Excitement bristles in the air.

Find a job or get on welfare.

Laughter. Then silence. The students settle back into overtime accounting and software. The part-time teacher sighs for the 60s.

THE PART-TIME TEACHER LEARNS HER STUDENTS WANT TO HEAL THEM-SELVES

The part-time teacher teaches a literature course in which local writers come to speak about their books.

Her students launch into a discussion on folk medicine after reading Joyce Carol Thomas's *Marked by Fire*. "Are there any Mother Barker's in the class?" the part-time teacher asks. Mother Barker is a root woman in *Marked by Fire*, a healer in the old-time African tradition.

One middle-aged woman, whom the part-time teacher always imagines as a young girl sitting in a large high chair swinging her legs, says her mother and grandmother were healers. "Why when we'd get hiccups, my mother would coil a string and stick it on our foreheads with spit, and we'd stop hiccuping!"

"Do you have the healing touch, too?" asks the part-time teacher hopefully.

"No," she says, "I need help!"

THE PART-TIME TEACHER DISCUSSES HER STUDENTS WHILE HER MATE SLEEPS

And do you know what Raquel did today? She tried to take over the class again and I had to. . . .

zzzzzzzzzzzzzzzzzzzzz

And do you know what Frank said? I couldn't believe it. He brought in a tape of William Burroughs. All I can remember is that section where he talks about soaking the American flag in heroin and smoking it, and everyone just sat there . . . Barbara was totally shocked. . . .

zzzzzzzzzzzzzzzzzzzzz

And then we had a big discussion on drugs. . . .

ZZZZZnort

III.

STUDENTS (INVOLUNTARY):

ENGLISH IA

THE PART-TIME TEACHER USES
THE PASSIVE VOICE

The long, dark semester trudges to a close. The sun sets. The last English IA composition is graded. The part-time teacher hopes that her students have finally learned today, in the second to last week of class, how to form the possessive of FATHER. She patiently says, "FATHER, add 'S to form the possessive of FATHER."

"What? What?" her students say. "Add S'?"

"NO. 'S FOR THE SINGULAR POSSESSIVE."

The genius of the class is getting bored; she writes like Herb Caen. The re-entry woman is also getting bored; she remembers her possessives from eighth grade. The part-time teacher is not bored. She is in possession of her chalk. "SNAP," it goes. Her hands are usually covered with fine dust at the end of class.

THE PART-TIME TEACHER SOMETIMES FEARS FOR HER STUDENTS' LIVES

The part-time teacher sometimes has her students read their English IA papers in front of class. She has not read them yet. She asks for volunteers.

A beautiful woman stands before the class and reads a paper in which she states that her husband beat her, and not only beat her, but hid in their house, and stalked her like prey in the jungle. The class is very silent, and she reads how she was pushed through a window, and forgave her husband in the hospital as blood streamed down her arm. She said she could not feel a thing; she had made herself a piece of wood, like Celie in *The Color Purple*, when Mr. beat her. She had made herself a piece of wood.

And she was white and middle class and had a good job, she said, and a child. And he was white and middle class and had a good job. Their friends all loved them as the perfect couple, and he stalked her at night if his socks weren't in a row in his drawer.

She saw a shrink who placed an image in her head. She was not wood; she was a pitcher of milk pouring out her contents. And he asked her how long her liquid love, her rich flowing milk could pour into her man — for her lifetime (which might be short), for a year, for a month? And she poured herself out till she was dry. It took a very short time. Then she left him.

The part-time teacher knows that some women write

to save their lives. The part-time teacher knows that some women speak to save their lives, and their sisters' lives.

THE PART-TIME TEACHER
TEACHES A UNIT FROM
THE BORZOI COLLEGE READER
CALLED "CULTURES IN TENSION"

She asks her English IA students to write an essay on the influence their ethnic background had on their upbringing. She asks them if they have ever been torn between two cultures.

A tall woman with dark hair reads her essay before the class. The part-time teacher thought perhaps the woman was Hispanic. She is not Hispanic. Her mother is Japanese, and her father is Caucasian. But her father left her mother when she was very young. Her mother raised her strictly Japanese. Everything was Japanese: Japanese church, Japanese school, Japanese friends, even a Japanese baseball team.When the young girl reaches high school, she has a growth spurt and is much taller than any of the other Japanese girls or boys in her school. The Japanese boys make fun of her and will not date her.

The Japanese woman standing at the front of the class reading her essay begins to cry. She tries to pull herself together, but the tears keep coming. She is nearly sobbing. "It was so horrible," she says. "They rejected me because I was part white. And I had always been Japanese." The part-time teacher wants to comfort the young woman. She tells her she doesn't have to finish reading her essay if she doesn't want to. But the woman insists on finishing her essay. She says she started dating a Caucasian boy who was kind to her. He helped build her self-esteem and now she is married to him. She goes back to her seat.

The part-time teacher feels deep within her soul the pain of a divided self. She is disturbed that white can be so hated, cause such pain for the children of mixed blood. What can she do? Should she beat her chest in guilt? For what, then? Because she herself was born with white skin? No, we do not choose our skin. We only choose our selves.

The young Japanese woman sits out the rest of the course in quiet and controlled dignity. She feels exposed; now she needs protection. The part-time teacher thinks *The Borzoi College Reader* should include another chapter: What do we do with the pain? What do we do with the wounds of the nation? What do we do with the wounds in ourselves?

THE PART-TIME TEACHER IS A WHITE WOMAN

On the first day of her English IA class, the part-time teacher sees a sea of dark faces. Only later does she separate their ethnic identities: 10 blacks, 10 whites, 2 Hispanics, 1 Indian (from India), 1 Filipino, 1 Eurasian. Why did she only see brown? Is she frightened?

The part-time teacher has a wonderful class for half the semester. The students are talkative, cheerful, and do their work. But soon she notices a few students' voices have begun to dominate the class. The part-time teacher wants to rectify the situation. She begins to call on the silent ones. They begin to say: "I haven't done the reading." Or they bullshit when they don't know the answer.

But when the discussion turns to issues that everyone can talk about without doing an ounce of reading, even the silent students pounce to speak. Male/female roles is a hot topic. Everyone wants to talk right down to the woman who denounces men for peeing all over the toilet. The Indian woman gives a women's rights speech that rouses her fellow students to clap. A black woman brings in an article published in *Ebony* called "The Necessary Bitch" written by a black woman trying to assert herself in a sexist and racist society.

The part-time teacher feels the class is primed to read

The Color Purple by a strong black woman. She is wrong.

THE PART-TIME TEACHER GETS IN HOT WATER TEACHING ALICE WALKER

The part-time teacher decides not to teach *Huckleberry Finn* this semester but to teach *The Color Purple*. Her classroom is half black so why not read some black literature instead of whitey stuff all the time?

A strong black woman in the class begins to denounce *The Color Purple* as an attack on the black man. Every day she hammers away at the book, at Alice Walker, and eventually at the part-time teacher. Her voice is so strong, her position so clear, that she intimidates any other voice in the class.

The part-time teacher decides to hold a mock trial. Is the book so controversial it should be banned from high school reading lists? During the trial, the strong black woman plays a high school student who's in favor of banning the book. In a mincing voice, she says she is a white girl from Marin, "And I think the book should be banned because isn't that what we whites think of you blacks already? That you're violent and you're rapists? We've heard the black man can't get a job, and after you read this book, you really won't want to give him one."

The black judge smashes down his gavel and asks what the other high school students think. He points at a black woman who is one of the most silent members of the part-time teacher's class. "What do you think?" he says. "I don't know," she says. "Don't you have any opinion on the book?" he asks. "No," she says. "And you," he gestures to a white woman. She says, "English teachers shouldn't teach books which deal with incest or sexuality; they should talk about terms like Omniscient Narrator and not deal with morals in the classroom."

The pro-*Purple* forces, including two black men, try to muster up an argument for the book, but they are cowed by the strong black woman's prowess and their own lack of preparation. Another woman in the anti-*Purple* forces says, "What if a white woman had written this book! Wouldn't you consider it degrading?"

The part-time teacher is shocked. The anti-*Purple* forces are accusing Alice Walker of being a white woman. The strong black woman says, "Some people are saying that the only reason this book got the Pulitzer prize is that it says what white people want to hear about us." As the argument goes on, the part-time teacher feels it is she herself who is on trial.

She is Alice Walker watching her book torn to shreds by a group of people who claim she isn't even speaking as a black woman. That she is racist for writing her own book. One of Celie's lines keeps racing through her head: "Somebody got to stand up for Shug." Somebody got to stand up.

"And another thing," says the strong black woman, "this book should only be taught by a qualified person with a background in Afro-American history."

The black class judge smashes down his gavel in imitation of Judge Wapner and decides against having the book taught in high schools. "On moral grounds," he says, "because of the lesbianism." "We didn't mention lesbianism," says a member of the anti-*Purple* forces. "I mean on account of the incest," he says. "And you," he motions to his cousin who is sitting in the pro-*Purple* camp, "you ought to be more prepared."

The class slinks off. The part-time teacher feels she has just been tried, convicted, and banished from the classroom for teaching a black book.

THE PART-TIME TEACHER DECIDES TO STAND UP FOR HERSELF

The part-time teacher drives home. She is angry. She wheels into a library and leafs through a book on banned books noting all the greats who've been banned: Socrates, Confucius, Joyce, Rabelais. She decides Alice Walker is in good company. She goes home and furiously types out all her arguments in favor of *The Color Purple*. She does not even know whether she will present them to her class, but it makes her feel better.

She goes into the classroom the next day. She looks out at her students' faces and decides YES. She must or her entire education will have been in vain. As soon as she opens her mouth, the strong black woman raises her hand and opens her mouth. "No," says the part-time teacher in a snappy tone. "This is my turn to speak." "Do you mean to say you are not allowing me to speak now?" "Yes," says the part-time teacher. She proceeds with her argument for *The Color Purple*. Her students sit and listen gravely to her words.

THE PART-TIME TEACHER PRESENTS HER FINAL ARGUMENT FOR *THE COLOR PURPLE* AND THE STRONG BLACK WOMAN RESPONDS

The part-time teacher asks her class a final rhetorical question: "Must the writer present role models for people in her work?" The part-time teacher confesses when she first became a feminist, she wanted writers to present strong role models for women in literature. She was sick of the Anna's, the Madame Bovary's, who committed suicide in the famous 19th century male novels, and the real life 20th century Anne Sexton's and Sylvia Plath's who did also.

But now, as a writer herself, the part-time teacher has come to the opposite viewpoint: that if the artist merely reflects what she thinks the public wants to hear, she will never have a vision. Alice Walker presents her vision; it may not be popular in the black community, but she speaks her own truth.

"Yes," says the strong black woman, "but we happen to be at a time in history when we can't afford to do that. We have to have role models. It would be wonderful if all artists could express what's in their hearts and souls, but we can't afford to do that."

"That's a terrible burden to place on an artist," says the part-time teacher.

"Yes," says the strong black woman.

THE WHITE PART-TIME TEACHER AND THE STRONG BLACK WOMAN HAVE AN EYE TO EYE CONFRONTATION

At the end of the class, the strong black woman marches up to the part-time teacher and says, "You've treated me terribly unfairly in rebuking me in front of the class. People have noticed that you treat me badly." "Uh oh," thinks the part-time teacher. "Here comes the lawsuit. Proceed with caution." But the part-time teacher is boiling and opens her mouth again. If she knows anything in life, it is what FAIR means. She is from a family of three girls and one boy. She knows what FAIR means.

"Have I treated you unfairly in this class? Haven't I given you your due every time you wanted to speak?" The strong black woman hesitates. It is the truth. The part-time teacher has called on the strong black woman more than anyone else in the entire class. "Well, I'm afraid you won't judge my work fairly now." "Your work is fine," says the part-time teacher.

The part-time teacher and the strong black woman stand looking at each other. For the first time, the part-time teacher sees small, etched lines on the strong black woman's forehead. "Ruth," she says, "we should be friends. We have a lot in common. We're both intellectuals. I just feel bad that here I am — whitey teaching Alice Walker — and I'm being accused of racism for doing it." The strong black woman smiles and says "Yes." "I'm a teacher, too," she says. "O, what do you teach?" says the part-time teacher. "Drug Abuse Counseling," she says, "to white men."

The part-time teacher sees the ultimate irony in their situations. "You know," says the part-time teacher, "you and I are carrying the tensions of the whole black/white conflict in this class. Everyone else is ducking their heads or hiding." And when she says this, the part-time teacher looks at the strong black woman and it's like looking into a mirror. Two teachers looking at each other, two role models, two perfectionists: the strong black woman trying to be the perfect role model for her race, and the white part-time teacher trying to teach the right liberal book at a third world school. The part-time teacher wonders whether the strong black woman buries her hostility toward whites every day at work as she must hide her fear of blacks when she comes to class.

The strong black woman and the white part-time teacher part with smiles. They are not smiles of friendship. They may be smiles of recognition, or they may only be smiles to cover up hostility. But somehow, the part-time teacher feels she has learned more from this one encounter with the strong black woman than from all the black books she has ever read.

THE PART-TIME TEACHER DEALS WITH MUTINY

The part-time teacher gives a C – to a little macho in her English IA class. He stomps up from his desk, crosses the front of the room while she is talking, and walks toward the door.

The part-time teacher says she wants to speak with him. "If you want to talk to me," he says, "you can come out here." He gestures with his finger to a spot on the floor. The part-time teacher waves her hand goodbye in disgust. She feels as if she might as well teach high school and forget about the pretense of college. She feels as if the spitballs will soon begin to fly. She feels as if the junior college ought to throttle junior before he's sent to class.

The little macho returns at the end of the hour. She is surprised. He apologizes. Says he spent more time on this paper than on his last one on which he got a B. But everything she says is correct, he admits. He cannot form possessives, and of course, he has run-on's, but he'll clean up his act. O.K.? He has the post-paper grunts and the shit-eating blues all at once. O.K., she forgives him with a silent reservation.

He becomes a model student, for a while at least, until the locker room brew at the back of the class makes him heady again with rebellion. The little macho emerges with potshot words and pint-sized ideas. The part-time teacher looks over his ears, won't play his game, but sizzles just the same.

THE PART-TIME TEACHER HAS A SCAM RUN ON HER

The part-time teacher tells her students that their papers are due on Monday, and if they are late, she will penalize them one grade.

On Monday, the classroom football hero comes in with a crutch. Everyone looks at him and inquires about his health. "It happens," he says with stoic dignity. At the end of the class, he hands her his paper in its usual battered plastic folder.

When the part-time teacher looks over her papers that evening, she notices that the football hero has given her his last week's paper that she has already corrected. Wednesday he shows up without his crutch and says, "I made a terrible mistake. I handed in the wrong paper Monday." He hands her another paper. "I noticed that," says the part-time teacher.

The part-time teacher thinks she has had a scam run on her: the crutch, the wrong paper, the grave mistake. It's the three card Monty of the classroom caper. But it's so beautiful, the part-time teacher decides not to question the maneuver. Besides, the football hero's first paper was an argument that jocks aren't dumb.

THE PART-TIME TEACHER ACCUSES A JOCK OF PLAGIARIZING

Excuse #1:
"When you told me I had a D in the course, I knew I had to do something," he says.

Excuse #2:
"I got four people to help me on this paper," he says. "Are you telling me I can't go to my resources and get help?"

Excuse #3:
"It took more than one person to build the atom bomb!" he says.

The part-time teacher finally understands what it means to have a whole ball team behind you.

THE PART-TIME TEACHER'S ENGLISH IA STUDENTS DISCUSS HOMOSEXUALITY

"I don't want them taking a shower with me," says the classroom jock.

"I don't want them rubbing off on me," says the ex-military man.

"RUBBING OFF ON YOU?" says a young, outspoken woman. "YOU'RE HOMOPHOBIC."

"What's that?". says the ex-military man.

"FEAR OF HOMOSEXUALITY."

"Well, I guess I have it!" he confesses.

"I'd rather be a drug addict than a homosexual!" says another classroom jock.

"Sometimes," says the older re-entry woman, "a person is homophobic because they fear being homosexual themselves. I don't mean that's the case back here," she says politely, waving her hand.

"My cousin is a homosexual," says the young, outspoken woman.

She swivels her head around and looks directly at the jock,

"and they don't want to (EXCUSE ME) fuck everything in pants!"

The part-time teacher doesn't know how her discussion on sex roles from *The Borzoi College Reader* got to this level so quickly. She needs an expert in the field at her side. She'd like to toss all her students into a class on human sexuality and prejudice. She'd like to be in it herself.

THE PART-TIME TEACHER OBSERVES A BLACK MALE AND WHITE MALE TESTING THEIR MACHISMO ON EACH OTHER

The part-time teacher has a very small English IA class with only thirteen students, and by mistake, the administration forgets to cancel it.

Two men are contenders for the center of attention in the class: one is white, the other is black. The white man is in his 20s; he is the only student the part-time teacher has seen at the college with a pony tail in the 80s. His parents were hippies. His step-father is a black man. Two weeks into the semester he cuts off his ponytail and claims he needs a writing therapist. He is constantly cutting up.

The black man is an actor. The part-time teacher lets him into her course on the basis of a paper he reads to the class. His sentences are dramatic, poetic; why he is a natural writer! She admits him to the class, collects his paper, and reads it at home. He writes in fragments; he can't spell the simplest words. The part-time teacher is mortified but can't go back on her decision. He sits in the front desk; he is constantly cutting up.

The two males spar on the subject of sex roles. The black male says, "My sister locked me out of the house and left me on the street when the bully was outside." The white male says, "I played house and dolls with my sisters, and my mother never put a stop to it. I always felt different." "Faggot! Faggot!" the black male whispers in the background.

The black male claims he is different. He says the theater director is prejudiced against him because of his POTENTIAL. The white male says, "Are you sure they're prejudiced against you because of your potential and not because of your skin color?"

They have a camaraderie of cutting up and cutting each other down. Neither is sure of his manliness, and they know it.

THE PART-TIME TEACHER IS HUNGRY

The part-time teacher has an older woman student from Nicaragua in her English IA class. She is shocked by American schools where the students can say "Fuck You" to the teachers. She tells the story of how teachers are respected in her country. She says when she was a little girl her mother made her carry a stinky chicken to school every Friday for her teacher. The part-time teacher is hungry. She wants the Nicaraguan to bring her a chicken every Friday even though she is a vegetarian. But the Nicaraguan woman gets a punk haircut, begins wearing bright red sweatshirts, and is busy buying a house in Pinole.

THE PART-TIME TEACHER HAS ADVANCED DEGREES AND NO IRA

The part-time teacher has students in strange and interesting jobs. One student markets furs to church-going women in Richmond. He wears a diamond stud in his ear. Another student runs a gold jewelry business. She wears a gold chain on her chest. A third is a tailor. A fourth works with computers in Safeway, and a fifth works with three and four year old children in a research hospital who have already gone through puberty.

The part-time teacher wonders why her students are taking English IA. She wonders why they are going to college if they already have decent jobs and are making more money than her. She wonders whether they will receive their degrees and then go back to marketing furs, selling gold jewelry, and working with computers. She wonders whether a B.A. stands for Back Action instead of Forward Motion.

THE PART-TIME TEACHER READS MELVILLE

When she first begins to teach, the part-time teacher reads a wonderful story by Melville called "Bartleby the Scrivener." The part-time teacher has just finished a long stint of clerical work. To her, Bartleby is an existential hero who says the very thing she wanted to say to all the magistrates who ever issued her the order:

"Will you type this letter?"

I PREFER NOT TO.

By the part-time teacher's third year of teaching, there are Bartleby's among her students, and she is the puzzled magistrate wondering what she can possibly do to motivate them, accommodate them, get them involved, do their homework, MOVE! They remain stubborn to the end: procrastinators, tardy, and unmoved.

THEY PREFER NOT TO.

"AH, HUMANITY! AH, HUMANITY!" the part-time teacher sighs, as she gives the Bartleby's of her beloved college their unearned C's and D's.

IV.

PERSONAL

THE PART-TIME TEACHER DOES NOT KEEP HORSES

The part-time teacher's answering machine says: "You have reached the message number for Arthur Korn, Landscaper, and Judith Wells, Writing Instructor." His friends ask him about horseback riding lessons and how much does she charge. They say she should pronounce "writing" more clearly and emphasize the T. She would like to dump a pile of manure on their heads.

THE PART-TIME TEACHER NEEDS A BENEFACTOR

The part-time teacher frets over her $200 Blue Cross payment that is coming up while her landscaper-lover wonders whether she's seen his $5,000 check that he's misplaced on the kitchen counter.

Later he returns from his guitar lesson, chuckling. "Andy sounds just like you," he says. "I forgot to bring my checkbook, and he's worried because he has a big insurance payment coming up." He chuckles. "Raise his salary," says the part-time teacher. "Give him a grant." "He doesn't want more money," says the landscaper-lover. "It's a tradition in the jazz world. Most master/pupil relationships are free."

Later he returns from a phone call. "Guess who that was. Andy. He needs $80 to make his rent this month. He's completely wiped out."

"Raise his salary," says the part-time teacher. "Give him a grant."

THE PART-TIME TEACHER MEETS A WOMAN IN THE WOODS WHO TELLS HER A STORY

The part-time teacher goes for a walk in the woods with her boyfriend to try to relax from the stress of her job. They meet a woman who tells the part-time teacher the following story:

"When I was 45, I went through my mid-life crisis and went back to school at a community college. I wanted to do the basics all over again from the start. My English IA teacher was great, but my math teacher was awful. I think it was probably the first time he taught. He had hair out to here, and his shirt was half off as if he had just come in from a fight. He didn't even look at anyone when he called the roll, and then he began putting formulas all over the board, from top to bottom. He bent over as he did it, and his hair went flying every which way. Not that I'm against hair or anything. Then a black woman in the back row said something to him, and they started a fight which went on all night. I said, 'Do I need this?' I could tell they were going to fight all semester, so I never went back. I think he was a sociopath."

The part-time teacher laughs hysterically. She has just had a hostile black woman in her classroom too, but she went through a whole semester before she got angry in class. The part-time teacher wonders whether she herself is a sociopath. She decides no. Someone simply wanted her power.

THE PART-TIME TEACHER IS EXAMINED WITH A FINE TOOTH COMB

The part-time teacher applies for another part-time teaching job and undergoes a stress test. She sits at a table with 8 other candidates for the job. They are to pretend they are a mutually supportive faculty trying to solve a teaching problem each one of them presents to the group. The administrators sit silently all around them, smiling discreetly, observing with hawks' eyes.

The part-time teacher's problem is the following:

"You have just been assigned a class and at the first session the students complain angrily about their last instructor. They mention he was disorganized, vengeful and irrational." Everyone laughs. "Sounds like a warning," says one man. "Assure them you're not like that," says one teacher. Another says, "Investigate! Take the teacher to task." Another says, "Carry on. Don't get involved. Tell them there're committees for student grievances." The part-time teacher juggles their suggestions and opts for "Carry on!" She'd rather teach than investigate, these days.

The part-time teacher comments brilliantly, she thinks, on other teaching problems: the student who dominates the course, the plagiarizer, the complainer about the work load, the terrible writers, the sexists, and racists. She has never been so sure of herself in a group in her life. Perhaps her three years of part-time teaching have not been in vain. It was all preparation for this stress test.

THE PART-TIME TEACHER BELIEVES THERE IS A CONSPIRACY AGAINST WOMEN'S POETRY CLASSES

The part-time teacher is scheduled to teach her women's poetry course at a community center in Berkeley. She is assigned a classroom next to a puppy training course. She protests but is informed that is all that is available.

On the night of the course she arrives with a huge stack of books and staggers up the walkway to the center in the pouring rain. She sees two of her friends who are taking the course walking away from the building. "They told us your course was cancelled," they say to the part-time teacher.

"What?" says the part-time teacher. She is outraged. She marches into the building. Puppies are dripping in the hall. She speaks to a tall, slim man in the office. "I was told your course was cancelled." "No it isn't," she almost yells. She collects her remaining students and marches down to her classroom. It is dark, cold, and dank. She sits in a circle with 12 women and a young man with a self-conscious moustache on his upper lip. He has come to collect the money from her students who haven't registered by mail. He urges them to pay up while the part-time teacher protests she hasn't even read them the syllabus yet.

He leaves saying he'll return next week. She breathes a sigh of relief and goes over her syllabus. When she gets to Sylvia Plath, a chorus of yip yips issues from the puppy room next door. The part-time teacher feels doom circling in the air.

The next week a blond woman comes to collect the remaining checks from her students. The part-time teacher hands her 5 checks. 8 weeks later, the course is over. The part-time teacher goes to collect her check from the college. The secretaries have no record that her course was taught. Their computer says she only had 5 enrollments, and her course was cancelled. The part-time teacher is shocked. She had 10 students. She looks through the files with the secretaries. No. checks were, ever processed. "Who'd you give them to," the secretary asks. "That blond woman," says the part-time teacher. "O, she was fired for absconding with funds." "Great," says the part-time teacher. Somehow, from the moment she heard about the puppy training class, she knew women's poetry was doomed.

THE PART-TIME TEACHER'S BOYFRIEND
TELLS HER SHE SHOULD
GET OUT OF THE SYSTEM
AND RUN HER OWN BUSINESS

The part-time teacher designs a home course for women writers and distributes her flyers around town in strategic bookstores and women's centers. She places a $50 ad in a magazine of Bay Area courses. Women begin to call her. They ask her if she is into the Tarot. She is not, particularly; she is into Sharon Doubiago and Sylvia Plath. Should she tell the truth?

A woman calls and says she does not have much money; could she trade massages for the course? The part-time teacher does not want a massage; she wants to pay the rent. Another woman wants to pay half-price for the first meeting so she can check the part-time teacher out. Women quiz her on her taste. Does she relate to John Ashbery? The part-time teacher does not relate to John Ashbery. She likes Susan Griffin and Judy Grahn. Should she tell the truth?

The part-time teacher spends many hours on the phone. She finally collects a group of women together who agree to meet on a certain Tuesday night at 7:30. She meticulously cleans her house, sends her boyfriend out, neatly stacks up her course material, and waits. At 7 o'clock a woman calls and says a good friend of hers has suddenly taken ill, and she must visit her in the hospital. But she will be there next week. At 7:25 a woman calls to say she cannot come; Oakland is too far from Berkeley, her home.

At 7:30 one woman shows up. The part-time teacher chats with her. She is also a part-time writing instructor. No one else shows up. The part-time teacher apologizes, cancels the class, and says she will be.teaching it again at Extension in the spring. The woman says she'd like to take the class then, but she's going to Nicaragua. She leaves. The part-time teacher decides not to run her own business.

THE PART-TIME TEACHER MEETS A
FELLOW TRAVELER

The part-time teacher applies to teach THE GREAT BOOKS at a Catholic college. She is asked to observe the class of "one of the finest instructors of the course." She calls him on the phone. The class is off campus in the basement of a hospital 20 miles from their homes, across a bridge. They decide to go together, and the instructor tells her: "I have a van with no heat, so if you want heat, we'd better take your car." The part-time teacher knows right away he is poor. But her car is 15 years old, and she too wants to conserve it, so she says; "I don't mind bundling up."

In his van, she finds out he has degrees in all kinds of things from all kinds of places. He wrote his dissertation in Germany in German and had it published. He also has a theological degree and used to be a poet when he had more time. He is writing a novel but he needs more time. The part-time teacher asks him whether he is trying to piece it all together with part-time teaching. Yes, he says. He has a class on Marx in San Francisco with only four students. How much does it pay? she inquires. 450, he sighs, only $100 a head, and does she know anyone who's interested in dialectical materialism? No, she confesses, but would he like to take a class in creative writing; she needs more students. He said he'd like to, but he doesn't have the time. He is teaching another course on rituals for the dead.

Do you meet many Ph.D.'s in your travels who are part-time teachers? she inquires. Yes, he confides. They are all at the Catholic college. He tears down the freeway on the rainy night like a man who knows his destiny is driving, and he's driving for his life and so is she.

THE PART-TIME TEACHER ASKS HER-SELF WHY SHE TEACHES PART-TIME

#1   Because she likes the money.

#2   Because she likes the hours.

#3   Because she truly loves her students, no matter what she says in these pages.

THE PART-TIME TEACHER
RE-EXAMINES HER ANSWERS WHY
SHE TEACHES PART-TIME

#1   Because she likes the money.
(Does she really like the money? Does she
often not end up making $5 an hour, especially
when she spends 8 hours correcting papers for
English IA? Is $5 an hour truly an adequate sal-
ary for a professional?)

#2   Because she likes the hours.
(Does she really like driving 15 miles on dark,
stormy nights to evening classes and teaching
from 7-10 p.m. and discussing Anne Sexton
and Herman Melville when most people
would rather be home watching football or
dozing off to sleep? Does she really like a 30
mile round trip commute for 1 hour of teach-
ing in the daytime?)

#3   Because she truly loves her students, no matter
what she says in these pages.
(No, sometimes she hates her students. They
get under her skin and tear at her innards.
There are days when she just wants to stay
home, and there she is, facing their faces. She
wants to put on a veil like the parson in Haw-
thorne's "The Minister's Black Veil." She'd like
to wear a Lone Ranger mask to class or a ski
mask. She'd like to carry a shield so when a
negative emotion comes flying out from a stu-

dent, she can raise her shield and watch the negativity slide to the ground and lie in a puddle at her feet. Sometimes she wishes she could disappear and still collect her pay.

Does the part-time teacher truly love her students?
Yes, the part-time teacher truly loves her students when they make her laugh, and when they speak so spontaneously from their lives and their souls that she is astonished that *they* do not wear masks (though they often are absent the next day). The part-time teacher, truly loves her students when she is weary, and they begin to encourage and appreciate each other. That is when she truly loves her students, especially the ones who dare to be themselves (yes, and who do their homework, too) and who empty out their souls like the woman who was prisoner at Auschwitz and who emptied out her memories in small clear poems with small clear words whose spaces in between told her pain, and like the grammar school teacher whose students once betrayed her and physically attacked her but who still teaches, because other children loved her, and who cried in the part-time teacher's writing class remembering, and the whole creative writing class felt her pain and loved her, and this is why the part-time teacher loves her students, and this is why she teaches.)

Rainy Day Women Press
is dedicated to publishing poems in the broadside
form. Catalogs are continually updated and
available on request. Broadsides begin at fifty cents
and usually remain at that price, however special
art editions might range from 75c to a dollar and
will be marked accordingly. We request a dollar for
postage on all orders. The publishers are devoted to
the issue of fine poetry and fine art.

This book was typeset by Pat Hunt in
Palatino 12 point type and printed by QED Press,
Fort Bragg, California

Rainy Day Women Press
Post Office Box 1085
Willits, California
95490